FOLLOW
YOUR
CURIOSITY

The uncharted path to your success

JOE PONI

Paperback: 978-1-7355377-0-2

Hardcover: 978-1-7355377-1-9

First paperback edition January 2020.

Edited by Dr. Elizabeth Naimbe

Cover art by Kenneth Ryan Monteclaro

Layout by HMDpublishing

I dedicate this book to you, Mom. When I became an author, I knew instantly I wanted to dedicate my first book to you. You have been the most significant source of inspiration, guidance, and encouragement throughout my life. I wouldn't be the man I am today without your love. Thank you for wisdom, support, and sense of humor. I am blessed beyond words to be your son.
I love you.

ACKNOWLEDGMENTS

Dad - Thank you for always believing in me and for all your support. You are the hardest worker I know. Thank you for showing me what sacrifice looks like. You have impacted my life greatly.

Gabriel - I have to give you a shout out because you always took the time to answer any question I had when I started my business. Thank you for being a great friend.

The Coffmans - You guys are the biggest dreamers I know. Lance, I am so grateful for our dream talks.

Matt & Des - You guys have been pivotal in my life. I love you dearly.

Cynthia - Thank you for taking a chance on me. I am indebted to you.

Nephews - Uncle Joe didn't know how to read until he was 18 years old. Today, I am an author. All things are possible to those who believe. Do your best in whatever you do. This book is for you. Uncle Joe loves you.

Benji - You are my greatest joy and happiest thought. I love you very very much. It is my honor to be your Dada.

Tanisha - May all your dreams come true, because all of mine were fulfilled being with you.

CONTENTS

INTRODUCTION

What you are about to read will change your life. The ideas presented in this book will lead you to opportunities that will make you happier, more successful, and give you a greater sense of purpose. I am proof. I went from not knowing how to read to a best-selling author. From no job to making six figures and finding the most fulfilling life to live. I have discovered my calling, gifts, and doubled my income working in a vocation I love by following the advice in this book. Your curiosity will be the pen that will design your future.

Here is who will find this book helpful:

- Those who are feeling stuck in life.
- Those trying to find out what career to pursue.
- Those facing multiple decisions that need help to decide a direction to go.

- Those who want to explore opportunities that will make them come alive.

Finally, if you want to impact the world, this book is for you. Do not miss your opportunity. This book provides a strategy that cuts straight to the point that will provoke you to think, take action, and share with others. In each chapter, I share personal stories, as well as those from successful entrepreneurs that will help inspire you on your journey. The chapters end with a "Strategy Session," that include action items to get you started. May this book inspire you to chart your own path, find your life's calling, and transform the world around you as you follow your curiosity.

PART 1:

EXPLORE & DISCOVER

CHAPTER 1:

FOLLOW YOUR CURIOSITY

*"Much of what I stumbled
into by following my curiosity
and intuition turned out to be
priceless later on." -Steve Jobs*

In 2015, I got fired while eating breakfast at a restaurant. I was a director of a small non-profit vocational school in Northern California, and at the time, the market was changing. The knot in the back of my throat got heavier as I got the news that I was being let go. I couldn't even finish my bacon. We had a business meeting at a restaurant and due to budget cuts, I couldn't stay on the books. My stomach turned as I thought about how I was going to tell my wife. I was the sole provider, so naturally my mind was racing: "Am I a failure?" "What will I do next?" "What comfort food could I eat for the next couple of days?"

When I came home and told my wife, although she was taken by surprise, she was very optimistic. She encouraged me everything would work out for the good and no matter what I chose to do next, we would be okay. As newlyweds, it was important for us to stay positive because we had just found out we were pregnant.

Within a week, I was able to get a new job, but it felt like a grind. Although I was thankful, I couldn't help but feel a sense of dread. Would I be stuck working at a job I didn't like for the rest of my life just to make a living? Knowing my son was on the way made me think about exploring a new path before he got here. I had nine months to find something I would enjoy doing that made me come alive. Where do I start? Should I go back to school? Should I start a business? I was facing some big decisions and didn't know which direction to go.

People are faced with these life-changing decisions every day – especially concerning their careers.

- What major should I pick?
- Is this the right job for me?

- Should I take this promotion?
- Should I start this business?

With so many options, making the wrong choice can feel like a waste of time. When you are stuck, people often tell you to, "follow your passion." But when you don't have a passion, this advice can feel despairing. And if you have several passions, this advice isn't helpful either. Passion is the result of exploration, discovery, then mastery. It isn't something you begin with or depend upon to figure out what path you should take in life. When it comes to finding what you are meant to do, the perfect place to start is to *follow your curiosity.*

Everyone is born curious. The desire to search, examine, and discover is the greatest sign of growth as infants. It isn't enough to present facts to a baby; they must taste, touch, and experience for themselves. Preschool children, on average, ask their parents about 100 questions a day[1] to explore their sense of wonder. But as children get older, they stop being curious. Immediate responsibilities, the cost of living and the pressure of rising prices, put people into survival mode.

The fiercely changing market has made playing it safe crucial. Following your curiosity can be discouraged by well-meaning parents, family members, and friends, because the possibility of failure is frightening. Stakes are high, and if you fail, who will rescue you? If you can't adapt, who will bail you out? Who will support you? To avoid casualty, people encourage finding your footing with a traditional, scripted life:

- Get an entry-level job
- Climb the corporate ladder
- Follow in line
- Don't rock the boat
- Work to retire

FIND YOUR PATH

This template is not a terrible idea – in theory. But as economies rise and fall, there are no guarantees. Since the 2008 Great Recession, traditional career paths have died as people lost their jobs, pensions, and 401ks. Those that made it through did so on pure grit alone. This tells me that the only safe path is the one you choose to take with conviction. Following your curiosity is permission to discover your own path. It is the freedom to find your destiny. Throughout history every inventor, innovator, explorer, and disrupter from The Renaissance to the 21st Century Digital Revolution was inspired by curiosity. As a result, they changed the world.

Sure, you will face failure along the way. But you will be amongst the greats – Kobe Bryant, Stan Lee, and Frida Kahlo, just to name a few. Sure, you will have missteps, but sometimes unexpected blessings come from mistakes. Afterall, Play-Doh, chocolate chip cookies, and the X-ray machine were all invented by accident. No one sets out to fail or make mistakes, but it does happen. When it does, an important part of the learning process is to be better. So, you cannot let the fear of failure paralyze you into living a mundane, unsatisfying life. You must courageously chart the course you are most fascinated with because that's where you will stumble upon your destiny.

> *Following your curiosity is permission to discover your own path.*

STEVE JOBS

Steve Jobs dropped out of college after his first year. He was a young man in search for more as he walked around, barefoot, and couldn't keep a job. He was carefree as he dabbled in electronics and sought spiritual enlightenment. Occasionally, he would drop by the Homebrew computer club, an early computer hobbyist group in Menlo Park, California, out of curiosity. Although Jobs wasn't the techie type, he was gifted with business instincts. He noticed the marketing potential of model-kit computers that you could assemble at home. To make quick cash, he shared a plan with computer enthusiast Steve Wozniak to create computer boards to local hobbyists. Their plan evolved when they approached The Byte shop, one of the first personal computer retailers, and a local store owner offered $500 for fully assembled computers. This is how Apple computers were born. When Steve Jobs stumbled into creating Apple, he didn't start with a passion, he started with a curiosity. That interest lead him to an opportunity that propelled him to his success. You never know where a simple suspicion will lead you or what it can turn into.

CURIOSITY LEADS TO OPPORTUNITIES

Curiosity is an invitation to explore, experience, and discover what fascinates you most. What makes you come alive? What makes you lose the sense of time? Curiosity will push you out of your comfort zone into a life that excites you. Sometimes curiosity comes in the form of a gut feeling or an inward nudge. Often times it starts with a thought:

- "Let's try."
- "That looks like fun!"
- "How does that work?"
- "This looks like an opportunity."

When you investigate your interests, they can lead to opportunities that were previously hidden. You may not know what the rest of your life will look like, but you can discover your next steps by pursuing your interests. You will be amazed where this single trait can take you. Take, for instance, Amazon's founder Jeff Bezos.

Bezos was working at an investment banking firm when he was caught off guard by the growth of the internet in the spring of 1994. In his 2010 speech at Princeton, he reveals "I came across the fact that web usage was growing at 2,300 percent per year. I'd never seen or heard of anything that grew that fast, and the idea of building an online bookstore with millions of titles - was very exciting to me." His interest of the growth of web usage led him to start an online company selling books. The rest is history. Start with your curiosity. This will provide you with a direction to take.

> *"When you're curious you find lots of interesting things to do."*
> *- Walt Disney*

MY JOURNEY

For as long as I can remember, I was always fascinated with making movies. As a kid, filming became a hobby after my brother brought home a camcorder. Growing up, I made free videos for friends and family who had weddings or events. I got my first paid side job when a friend told me he hired someone to film a business video for his company. I told him I would make a better video for half the price. So, he canceled his first choice and hired me. I blew him away. But I never considered filming as an option for work because the only filmmakers I knew of were in

Hollywood. But then the tech boom changed everything. Companies sprouted up all over Silicon Valley, and businesses were turning to video to market their content online. This opened the door for videographers who could produce professional videos. Around that time, I came across a statistic that showed the future of internet traffic will be predominantly video,[2] and companies everywhere were jumping on board. This was my invitation. My interest found an opportunity.

I asked my wife if I could invest our savings into production equipment to start a business. Although we barely had enough to get by and buy groceries, she was very supportive. I promised that if the business didn't work by the time Benji (our son) was born, I would find "a real job." Together, we took the leap. It was scary and uncomfortable, but I didn't have time to be afraid. I didn't know what I was doing most of the time, but I was motivated. The bitter feeling of not being able to buy all the groceries we wanted because we didn't have enough money compelled me to succeed. Thankfully, that first year, our business worked. Not only did we make it, I did better than we thought. I went from not having a job to owning a video production company that went on to make six figures. I have done commercial work with Google, LinkedIn, Facebook, and Shark Tank. By following my curiosity, I joined millions throughout history who found a path that made them come alive.

THE PERFECT PLACE TO START

Whether you are looking for a career, currently employed, or in need of an adventure, following your interests will make you come alive. Even if you have countless options before you, but simply don't know where to begin, a perfect place to start is in the direction of your greatest curiosity.

You will be amazed by what you find.

STRATEGY SESSION

1. TAP INTO YOUR CURIOSITY

Your interests are what make you unique. Some fascinations can be temporary, while others can lead you to lifelong bliss. It all depends if you like what you find as you poke around and follow your curiosity. Most of us do not know what we like or dislike until we get out of our comfort zone and try it. As I look over my life, I have become most successful in the things that I was most interested in:

- Making movies on my camcorder for my family and friends to watch
- Speaking
- Making people laugh
- Standing up for others

I had no idea I would go on to become a filmmaker, businessman, minister, public speaker, among others. I just followed my interests, and they led me to a road of enjoyment. Here are some questions to help you create your compass:

- What are you most fascinated about?
- List the things you always wanted to try.
- What is the latest opportunity you have seen that aligned with your interests?

Finding your place in the world starts by taking one step at a time in the right direction. If you were looking back on your life, would you regret not doing something? If so, what is holding you back?

2. DO MARKET RESEARCH

In order to increase your chances for success, do some market research. Are there potential growth opportunities in the market that fascinate you? We learned how Steve Jobs saw marketing potential with computers and pursued that opportunity. Jeff Bezos was fascinated with the internet and started his online business. I discovered a statistic that the future of internet traffic would be predominantly video and took a leap of faith. What does the market predict for the near future? Using your skills or experiences, how can you position yourself for success?

3. DEVELOP A CONCRETE PLAN

Take a look at your schedule. Is there time you can set aside in the morning or after work to dive deeper into your curiosities? Can you make time for yourself to reflect, dream, and explore your interest? Is there anyone you can reach out to that is doing something inspiring that you can meet? (See Chapter 6 for how to set up meetings.) Start a budget for personal research and development. Reserve that money for new experiences that will help you grow as a person.

You only get one life to live, don't waste it being too busy.

4. BREAK OUT OF YOUR COMFORT ZONE

Life is exciting when you're exploring, learning, and making a dent in the universe. When life gets boring and predictable, you have to look in the mirror and see if you have become complacent. Living in a comfort zone has a way of sapping the enthusiasm out of you until you live an apathetic life. Your greatest work and experiences will happen outside of your comfort zone. Eleanor Roosevelt once said, "Do one thing every day that scares you." If regularly doing something that scares you is unrealistic for your schedule, make it a habit to do something outside of your comfort zone once a week. Challenge yourself to meet new people, learn different cultures, travel to different places, or even order something new on the menu. Become curious about things you haven't experienced before. Get rid of your excuses: I'm too old for that. It's a bad time right now. I don't have the time. If you don't have the time, make the time. You won't be disappointed.

And if you don't want to do it alone, get a friend to go with you!

CHAPTER 2:
RE IMAGINE YOUR POSSIBLITIES

*"You must do the thing you
think you cannot do."*
- Eleanor Roosevelt

Yessi is a friend of mine who was a college graduate that majored in business and lived in a small city in central California. By the time she was in her thirties, she was responsible, successful, and had a promising career. Wherever Yessi went she was the life of the party because of her vibrant personality and her sense of humor. You would have never guessed she felt miserable. Although her job gave her financial stability, deep down she was unhappy and unfulfilled with her place of work. That void led her to reimagine what her life could look like. She started to investigate what she was most interested in and what she found transformed her life.

For most of society, when it comes to finding a job, happiness isn't high on the list; financial security is. As a result, weekdays become a blur. Life is reduced to waiting for the weekend and just living for a paycheck. Concerning this, author Henry David Thoreau, the great American poet wrote, "the mass of men lead lives of quiet desperation." Quiet desperation is the feeling you have when you go through life taking care of responsibilities, but deep down you find yourself dissatisfied and unfulfilled. The thought of freedom isn't realistic when you have bills, children, and commitments. If you are unhappy working at a job and feel stuck, there is hope. What if you could find security and happiness doing something you were interested in? In today's climate, anything is possible. You just need to know how to look.

In the age of technology, new jobs that no one ever anticipated are sprouting up at an accelerated pace. A 2016 World Economic Forum report found that, "in many industries and countries, the most in-demand occupations or specialties did not exist ten or even five years ago, and the pace of change is set to accelerate."[3] In other words, technology is moving at such a rapid speed, your dream job may not even exist yet! There are exciting careers available now and new jobs on the way. Your responsibility is to be aware of your interests, skills, and personality to find the right fit.

Yessi's misery pushed her out of her comfort zone into exploring her curiosity. She was interested in several things:

- Making people laugh
- Helping people
- Personal development
- Living in San Diego, CA
- Dancing

The first thing she did was sign up for a comedic school and did stand-up comedy in her free time. Yessi became a crowd favorite. Unbeknownst to her, this helped her build up her risk-taking muscle, which empowered her to follow her curiosity. She loved helping others, so she signed up for a two-week mission trip to do humanitarian work in Romania. When her job refused to give her the deserved time off, she quit and left for Romania anyway. When she came back, unemployed, she had time to find the right job for herself. She took into account her interests, skillset, and the lifestyle she wanted to live. When a friend referred her to a job that was located in her dream city, San Diego, California, she was more than excited to accept. Being new to town, Yessi thought she should put herself out there, so she joined a beginner Bachata dance team, where she met her roommate. She was then invited to her roommate's birthday dinner, where she ended up meeting her future husband. Looking back, Yessi knows that had she not followed her curiosity to comedic school, she wouldn't have found the courage to follow her heart that led to her dream city and dream guy. Once you reimagine what life can be, without society's narrative and fear of failing, you start designing your own story. Investigating your interests can lead to true satisfaction and happiness.

EVALUATE YOUR DEFINITION OF SUCCESS

What does success look like to you? Your perception of success will dictate your lifestyle. Success should be what makes you happy, not the thing that makes you look happy. If you ask 10 people on the street what success is to them, they will all have different answers. You are free to define what success looks like for yourself. If it is to be rich, be rich! If it is to drive a fancy car, get one! Whatever your definition of success is, you should always be able to answer why it is success to you. Because if you think living a fancy life will make you happy, I can point you to many people who are rich but unhappy. Just because you want to be a millionaire doesn't mean you have to look like it. Most millionaires live frugal, below their means, and value financial independence more than displaying high social status.[4] You must be careful not to live someone else's definition of success. More possessions and social status will not fill your void or give you peace. I have found that true success is peace. The lifestyle that will give you peace is the right fit for you.

What does success look like to you?

PLAN OF ACTION

Making the jump into a new lifestyle can be daunting at any age. As a young person, you may lack resources. However, youth gives you the freedom to explore without great financial responsibilities. As you get older, taking risks can be difficult when you have commitments and bills. Nevertheless, you have the capability to figure out a way to do what you need to do. Whatever your situation may be, you will never make it if you are not desperate for a change. You must have a plan of action. If you are looking to change careers, start setting aside money to make your leap. It wouldn't be wise to immediately quit your job before you found another one just because you realized what you want to do. You have to set yourself up gradually before you transition. When I became an author, I was running a video production business and fulfilling all my other roles and commitments simultaneously. I wrote every night for three months from 9 p.m. until midnight. Pursuing your interests will not come without upfront sacrifice. You must make the time and work hard for it.

STRATEGY SESSION

1. KNOW YOUR STRENGTHS

What are your gifts? What are your skills? In his book, *Strengths Finder 2.0*, Tom Rath states, "Far too many people spend a lifetime headed in the wrong direction. They go not only from the cradle to the cubicle, but then to the casket, without uncovering their greatest talents and potential." Most people do not know what they are good at. When you discover your gifts and strengths, you uncover areas of work where you can build upon and excel. The more self-aware you become, the more successful you will be in finding a career that works for you. Here are some questions to help you identify your gifts and strengths. Feel free to list multiple answers for each question.

- Where have you seen the greatest success without much effort?
- What do you love doing that comes naturally?
- List the jobs and hobbies you have had in the past. What talents did you acquire from these experiences?
- What are some of the ways you can grow in your gifts? Can you sign up for a seminar? Take an online course? Find a mentor?

2. DREAM JOB

There are a lot of career options in today's market. Finding a job that you enjoy, that gives you meaning, while utilizing your gifts, is what many consider a dream job. Most "dream jobs" require training, education, or lower-level entry jobs to start. What industry interests you? If you could work at any job, what would it be? What is so interesting about your ideal work environment? What skills do you have to offer? Please fill out the graph on the next page to help you identify your ideal job.

WHAT INDUSTRY INTERESTS YOU?	JOBS YOU WOULD LIKE TO WORK IN THIS INDUSTRY	WHAT IS YOUR PEAK INTEREST?	WHAT SKILLS OR GIFTS DO YOU HAVE TO OFFER?
EXAMPLE: Tech industry	Facebook headquarters, LinkedIn headquarters	Creative work environment. Great food. Work that is meaningful to the world. Having fun	Speaking, problem solving, helping people feel at peace in high-stress situations, creativity, coding.

On your graph, look for commonalities or places where these descriptions might overlap. Do you have similar peak interest for different jobs? Do you have similar skills that can be used in different industries? Are you willing to learn new abilities? A common thread may help open you up to more creative career options. What plan of action can you develop to step into your ideal career?

3. FIND YOUR ENGAGEMENT

Professor Mihaly Csikszentmihalyi conducted a study to understand where in everyday life people feel the happiest. He studied artists, scientists, and people from all walks of life. What he discovered is that the happiest people are the ones who find their "flow." When you are in the "flow," you are in the zone. You are completely engaged and sense a feeling of ecstasy. Time goes fast as you experience complete focus and enjoyment. When you find activities that make you feel engaged and energized, you are on the right track. Do any of your interests make you lose sense of time? If you have a sense of engagement in your life, start looking into your interest to find your flow. One interest can lead you to opportunities you could have never imagined.

4. PLAN YOUR ESCAPE

Oxford languages defines a career as, "an occupation undertaken for a significant period of a person's life and with opportunities for progress." The average worker spends 50 years employed.[5] With so much time dedicated to a career, it would be a disaster if you didn't do what you enjoyed. Working at a job you don't like just because it pays well is not a reason to stay. If you desire to transition into a new profession or career, it will take a good plan and self-discipline. Start by saving at least four months of expenses. Cut back on eating out to put money aside to invest in your dream. Choose to live on a budget. Dedicate time each day you can work toward your interest. Stay up the extra hours. It will be hard, scary, and uncomfortable. But you can make the leap if you believe in yourself. Do everything you can to set yourself up to make a successful jump. The life you want to live is waiting for you.

5. IMAGINE YOUR LIFESTYLE

Your career isn't your whole life; it's just one piece of it. Other areas such as health, values, faith, family, and friends are just as important, if not more. How many people have missed out on all these other parts of life because they were so consumed with their jobs? Your life shouldn't revolve around your career. Your career should revolve around the life you want to live. Here are some questions to consider when imagining the lifestyle that you want:

- How much flexibility do I want with my schedule?
- How do I want my family time to look like?
- What is the limit of intensity that I want in my job?
- What do I want my social life to look like?
- What do I need for my mental and physical health?
- What do I want to be known for?

Imagining the life you want will shape your career choices. And your definition of success will shape your lifestyle.

CHAPTER 3:

YOU ARE NOT BEHIND IN LIFE

"Eventually everything connects." -Charles Eames

I felt behind in life. People from high school were off to their dream careers, buying houses, getting married, and having kids. Things weren't clicking for me as fast as they seemed to be for everyone else. I was still wondering where to take my place in the world. There is an unspoken timetable society has that if you are not on that track by a certain age, people start to get worried.

My relatives would ask questions like:

"What do you want to do with your life?"

"Are you going to go back to college?"

"When are you going to get a nice girl?"

Then, when I found a nice girl, they asked: "When are you going to get married and have kids?" I quickly realized I didn't fit along society's timeline. The more I listened to the beat of my own heart, the more I started to get comfortable with my expression of life.

After I graduated high school, I went to college and worked as a secretary at a business in San Francisco for my uncle. I wanted to experience corporate life in the city. Around that time, I became a public speaker in high schools, traveled overseas, and built homes for the less fortunate in Mexico. I filmed as a hobby, mentored youth, took mission trips, went to a vocational school, and eventually became the director of it. I also worked at my dad's construction company to make some side cash. I became more self-aware with each experience. I figured out what I liked and didn't like. I discovered what I was good at and what I wasn't. I naturally gravitated toward the things I liked and cultivated skills in those areas. Eventually, I became a filmmaker, and today I am an author.

You may read my journey and get the impression that I knew what I was doing all along. I didn't. I just followed my greatest interest, and it led to my success. If I failed, I failed forward by doing my very best. The path to success isn't a straight line. It is messy and all over the place. However, if you do your best in whatever season you find yourself in, you increase your chances for your success, even if it is not where you think you should be.

MR MIYAGI

There is a powerful scene in the movie *The Karate Kid*. The main character, Daniel, wanted to learn karate to defend himself from the kids at school who bullied him. One day, Daniel met a man named Mr. Miyagi who vowed to teach him karate. During his first lesson, Mr. Miyagi had Daniel clean his cars. He showed Daniel precise movements: "Wax on... Wax off..." Although Daniel was initially thrown off, he obliged for the chance to learn karate. After he finished cleaning an old collection of automobiles, Mr. Miyagi showed him how to sand his floor, then paint his fence with precise movements: "Side to side...and...up and down..."

When Daniel got frustrated with Mr. Miyagi about not teaching him karate, Mr. Miyagi asked Daniel to do the "Wax on... Wax off..." movement while he threw an unexpected punch. To Daniel's surprise, he blocked Mr. Miyagi's punch. Then, Mr. Miyagi asked Daniel to paint the fence while he threw another punch. Once again, to Daniel's surprise, he blocked Mr. Miyagi's punch by using the technique he learned from painting the fence. The point of the lesson was that everything you experience is preparation for where you are going in life.

EVERY EXPERIENCE IS PREPARATION

Looking back, when I followed my interest, every experience and failure I had prepared me for my next season. Even during moments when I felt out of place. I look back at these times and realize I found wisdom, learned a lesson, or picked up a valuable skill. It was not a waste of time at all! You may have a job you don't like and assume it has nothing to do with your destiny. Take heed, every moment – good or bad – can work for your purpose later on down the road. Don't be distracted by those on social media who look like they are further along. Their lives have nothing to do with your story. Stay focused on your goals and your process. Have patience with yourself. Don't be in a hurry to abort the process. Look for the hidden treasure. What can you learn? Who can you meet? Do not be so focused on the future or what you don't have that you miss the blessings right in front of you.

Everything you experience is preparation for where you are going in life.

GIVE IT 100%

As you follow the beat of your heart and your interests, keep in mind that you will not be successful if you only put in 70% - 90% effort. You must give 100% in each decision you make. Show up on time, be professional, put in the hard work, and don't miss the days. If you make a decision that turns out to be the wrong thing, it will serve as a launching pad to get you into the right thing. You never know who was watching you work, who you will meet along the way, or what skills you will learn that can lead to an opportunity down the road. When you give your best, even in bad times, it can still lead you in the right direction.

Sadly, too many people are paralyzed with indecision. In his book *Facing the Enemies Within,* Jim Rohn says: "Indecision is the thief of opportunity and enterprise. It will steal your chances for a better future." Making no decision is still making a decision, just without results and data to work with. In the scientific community, when things don't work, it isn't called a failure; it is called an experiment. The more experiments you take on, the more opportunities you attract. Everything you experience can be used to help you.

SEASONS OF LIFE

Just like there are seasons in nature, there are also seasons in life. Just as spring turns into summer and fall prepares the Earth for winter, your experiences in each season are preparing you for the next. If you ever feel stuck, unnoticed, or frustrated, you must remember that things will spring forward, blossom, or fall off and evolve. You must remind yourself that if your current season isn't comfortable, it isn't a life sentence. It won't always feel like winter. Spring is coming. Your job is to take full advantage of whatever season you find yourself in, no matter how long it feels, knowing it is preparing you for your destiny.

STRATEGY SESSION

1. GAIN EXPERIENCE

During career sessions in high school, I would always feel anxious because I didn't know what I wanted to do for work. Peers would share they were going to be nurses, real estate agents, and graphic designers, but I sat clueless. The traditional approach to a career was to pick something you wanted to do for the rest of your life. And with the retirement age rising, that is a big decision to make if you have no experience or are uncertain about what to do.

If you're like me, you may need time to explore what you like and what you don't like. How else will you stumble into what you would want to do? Let's start with your greatest curiosities. You can start a business, work at different jobs or careers, and after you gather those experiences, you can target where you want to be. When the opportunity comes up where you want to work, you will know for a fact that's where you want to be. Then you can apply all your energy toward it.

"Twenty years from now, you will be more disappointed by the things you didn't do than by the ones you did do. So throw off the bowlines. Sail away from the safe harbor. Catch the trade winds in your sail. Explore. Dream. Discover." **-Mark Twain**

2. STAY AWAY FROM COMPARISON

Allow yourself the chance to experience life without the pressure of feeling like you should be further ahead. Don't judge yourself by someone else's life. You are not on society's timetable. You are running your own race.

Have social media played a part in making you feel behind in life? If you are tempted to compare your life with others, take a break and unplug. Comparison will steal your joy. If you feel the temptation of comparison on social media, take a moment to mute, unfriend, or take a break from that platform or from those people. Protect your mental health and focus on yourself.

3. ENJOY THE SEASON YOU ARE IN

The best season of your life is the current season you are in. Do not be so focused on the future that you miss the blessings of your current season. Take a look around you, are there any hidden treasures you can find? What can you learn? Who can you meet? What are 10 things you are grateful for in your life right now? Write them down to cultivate gratefulness in your current season of life.

PART 2:

CULTIVATE &

EXECUTE

CHAPTER 4:

DISRUPTERS

"It always seems impossible until it's done." -Nelson Mandela

Today, we are at the dawn of another revolution. We are surrounded by technology that is changing the world at an accelerated rate. Artificial intelligence, biotechnology, virtual reality, augmented reality, and robotics are all manifesting at the same time. We are seeing the future unfold right before our eyes. As the world evolves, disruption will put millions of people out of work, but it will also provide millions of new jobs. The force of innovation and competition creates relentless change in the global market and every industry, business, and worker will need to find new footing. How do you find your place in the world? How will you stand out in the market's next wave? Whether you are an entrepreneur or an employee, your ability to adapt and provide value is essential to standing out. Those who bring innovation and design solutions will become irreplaceable.

Kenneth Clark, an art historian, referred to Leonardo Da Vinci as "the most curious man in history." Da Vinci is known for his inventions, engineering, philosophy, architecture work, science, drawings, and paintings. His creativity is world-renowned 500 years later! Da Vinci refers to the secret behind his genius as "Saper Vedere." Which means "knowing how to see." How is your "Saper Vedere?" Do you see through the lenses of limitation and restriction or through the lenses of imagination and wonder? Perception can be either your superpower or your disability. Knowing how to see is the ability to envision beyond what exists and imagine what can be. Innovation can be ignited from anything. While frustrations and laziness serve as pain points to some, to those that "know how to see," it can be an opportunity. For example, between 1936-1938, a German engineer, Konrad Zuse, built the first programmable digital computer. His motivation for building the device was, "I was too lazy to calculate, and so I invented the computer." Basically, the first digital computer was birthed from laziness.

WHEN ELON MUSK IS BORED

Elon Musk has revolutionized the world with his forward thinking and his ability to generate solutions. He created multibillion-dollar companies like Tesla Inc., Neuralink, and SpaceX. The secret to his success, undoubtedly, is not only hard work, but his ability to use imagination in everyday life, even when he gets bored.

It was 5 a.m. on December 17, 2016, when Musk was stuck in traffic on the Los Angeles 405 freeway when he had a thought. As he sat there, he envisioned "Hyperloop" tunnels underneath the city of Los Angeles that could get someone across town within minutes. He not only thought of this idea in traffic, but he had time to tweet about it.

5:05 a.m. December 17, 2016: "Traffic is driving me nuts. Am going to build a tunnel boring machine and just start digging…"

He followed up this tweet at 7:15 a.m. by tweeting, "It shall be called "The Boring Company."

Your perception can be your superpower or your disability.

Not only did he follow through by creating "The Boring Company," but he successfully built a prototype of the Hyperloop under his SpaceX parking lot. He was able to create tunnels for hundreds of millions of dollars cheaper than expected. The next time you feel bored at work, don't pick up your phone, pick up an idea.

You don't have to have a light bulb moment to solve problems or be innovative. From the examples above, you can feel lazy, frustrated, or weary of traffic! You may not develop the next computer or build a tunnel under your house, but you can provide value at your workplace by implementing innovation.

DISRUPTERS

The irony of today's market is every company needs change to be competitive, and yet people don't like change. It's too disruptive. Providing value in your workplace is not only creating solutions or suggesting ideas but communicating them in a professional way to get the team on board. Having great ideas gives you the chance to be an asset to any organization. This is how you showcase value and grow in a company. When you are dependable, innovative, and easy to work with, you provide value. Your demeanor, punctuality, posture, the way you conversate, keep eye contact, break the ice, use humor in the right context, all adds to the value. The more value you can provide, the more irreplaceable you become. Thinking outside the box and challenging the status quo are attributes of disrupters. Disrupters do not see problems; they see opportunities.

Have you ever asked, "Why isn't anyone doing something about this?" This is a great clue that you are the perfect candidate to do something about it. You have already identified a problem. The next step is to propose a solution. It takes collaboration and effective communication to see a solution come to pass. You may be the agent of change to help.

Have you ever thought, "This could be done better"? This usually indicates that something can be done faster, easier, or more conveniently. Henry Ford's assembly line transformed the world. What made Ford stand out at that time was not the Model T, but the innovative way he found to make cars in a shorter amount of time. He was simply able to do it better.

*Disrupters do not see problems;
they see opportunities.*

SERVING OTHERS

The fastest way to innovation is being mindful of the needs of others. The ability to empathize and serve others not only provides value, but also leads to a great life. Martin Luther King Jr. put it like this, "Everybody can be great... because anybody can serve. You don't have to have a college degree to serve. You don't have to make your subject and verb agree to serve. You only need a heart full of grace. A soul generated by love."

One of disrupters' greatest attributes is having a mindset of serving others. Some of the most impactful leaders and entrepreneurs are servants. Businesses that adopt service missions become more profitable than those just focused on profit. Take, for instance, Blockbuster.

At one point, Blockbuster employed 84,000 people worldwide and made 5.9 billion in one year in revenues.[6] Most of its profits came from charging late fees.[7] Although late fees were good for profits, they were horrible for customer experience. Everyone hated late fees – especially Reed Hastings. One night, Reed dropped off his movie rental and had to pay a $40 late fee. Out of his frustration, he had an idea. He thought of a convenient service that had unlimited rentals and no late fees. This idea gave birth to Netflix. By implementing superior customer service, Netflix eclipsed Blockbuster. The rest is history.

You do not have to start a business to serve others. You can be an asset wherever you go by simply being a great helper. Do you have friends that own a business you can support? Do you know someone who has a dream you can help?

Just asking others, "How are you doing? Is there anything I can help you with?" goes along way. Serving others gives meaning to life.

After the U.S. Civil War, cotton crops started to diminish. The economy in Southern states began to decline. One man by the name of George Washington Carver saved the South's economy with solutions and innovative thinking. Dr. Carver was an African-American agricultural scientist and inventor who became world-renowned for his work inventing over 300 uses for peanuts. According to the Missouri Department of Agriculture, "Dr. Carver and the peanut helped save the economy of the southern part of the U.S. Alabama residents saw cotton oil mills converted to produce peanut oil. This was something that farmers could thrive on – livestock could eat the peanut plant and sharecroppers could feed their families on crops that weren't sold." In the midst of racism, he promoted racial harmony. In a time of collapse, he helped people prosper. Because of his innovative thinking, Dr. Carver saved the South. Society is yearning for change agents to do something. Industries are in need of people who provide solutions. What can you do? Who can you serve? Don't be afraid to be the instrument for transformation at work, home, or in society. If you experience a pain point, you may be the agent of change to do something about it.

YOU ARE NOT MEANT TO SOLVE ALL THE WORLD'S PROBLEMS

In order for you to be effective in life, you must give up the messiah complex. Your goal shouldn't be to solve all the world's problems. Your goal should be to solve *your* world's problems. This doesn't mean you turn a blind eye to what's happening around the country or globe. This just means you release yourself from the burden of saving the whole world. Your focus should be to take care of what is in front of you and what you feel called to do.

STRATEGY SESSION

1. DEVELOP YOUR PERSPECTIVE

The secret to Da Vinci's genius was "Saper Vedere," "knowing how to see." How do you see
the current challenges around you? Do you see
through the lenses of limitation and restriction
or through the lenses of imagination and wonder? How do you see yourself? Are you critical
or do you believe in yourself? On a scale of 1-10,
how empowering is your perspective? Could
it use an upgrade? The key to transformation
comes through renewing your mind from negative thoughts to empowering thoughts. Every
problem turns into an opportunity when you
see through the lens of imagination and wonder. Take a look at your biggest obstacle right
now. Exchange a bleak perspective with one
filled with hope. This is how you elevate your
"Saper Vedere."

2. PROVIDE VALUE

Whether you are meeting the needs of consum-
ers or being an asset at your place of work, long
term success hinges on your ability to provide
value. Everyone defines value differently. What
is considered valuable to one, may not be valuable to another. Therefore, your job is to figure
out what is important to the people/organiza-
tion you serve and meet those needs through

your attributes and creativity. The more value you provide, the more valuable you become in the marketplace.

Take a moment to think about the current workflow at your workplace. Does the thought, "There must be a better way" or "Someone should do something about that" ever cross your mind? Every pain point has an opportunity hidden within it. Can you be the agent of change to bring a solution? If so, disrupt the status quo.

3. USE YOUR VOICE

Jim Rohn once said, "You don't get paid by the hour. You get paid for the value you bring to the hour." If you bring value to your workplace but feel undervalued, you may need to summon the courage to share what you need to your supervisor. Whether it be shift change or hourly raise, stating what you need will put you on your supervisors' radar. If you feel nervous, keep note of your achievements and the value you bring to the team. This way, if you ever need to share why you deserve what you are asking for, you have a record to justify your needs. Be bold. Be you. Bring value and use your voice.

CHAPTER 5:
UNLOCK YOUR CREATIVITY

"Everybody is a genius. But if you judge a fish by its ability to climb a tree, it will live its whole life believing that it is stupid."
-Albert Einstein

Everyone is creative. You may not consider yourself creative, but you are. Just because you don't finger paint or make graphic designs doesn't mean you are not artistic and creative. I define creativity as taking what is unseen in your imagination and making it reality. That can be a report, rearranging a room, getting ready in the morning, taking a photo, putting up decorations, etc. No matter how simple or elaborate an action is, if you are creating something or making something better, you are using creativity.

Quite often, people find it difficult to tap into their inner genius because they don't see themselves as creative. Criticisms, judgments, doubts, and fears sap people's inner genius.

Professor George Land gave an amazing TED talk on creativity.[8] In it, he shared how he led a research study of 1600 children under the age of 5. This study was to test students who possess genius-level skills, which he says is the ability to "look at a problem and come up with new, different, innovative ideas." Ninety-eight percent of those children from the ages of 4-5 scored genius level. They retested the same children at 10 years old and discovered the proportion that were genius level went down to 30%. After five more years, at age 15, only 12% of children excelled at creative thinking. The same test was given to over 200,000 adults and found only 2% operated at genius level. What happened? The study showed that as people aged, the more they heard "no, that can't be done," or "this is impossible," and began to believe it. Judgments and criticism sapped their inner genius. Creativity is suppressed when you accept negative comments. The good news about this study is that creative genius still was still dormant in every adult they surveyed - "just waiting to break free."

BE CHILDLIKE

The first step to rediscovering your creative genius, according to George Land, is to practice divergent thinking. In other words, use your imagination and be childlike. In his book, *Break-Point and Beyond*, George Land details how this is done: "Retaining or recapturing the simple playfulness of a child opens a person up to creative possibilities. Listen to music, finger-paint, wear a crazy hat, make a face, dance, monkey around, talk to yourself, fiddle, scream, yell at the moon. Recapture your child-like nature." While adults are often serious, uptight, reserved, and burdened by the weight of adulthood, children are carefree and full of life. Kids do not think in terms of embarrassment or fear of failure. Children do not consider impossibility either. There is always a creative suggestion or rebuttal to bypass the word "can't." When was the last time you used your imagination and creativity? What activities listed above can you do to recapture your child-like nature? Maybe it is time to exercise your creativity.

"The true sign of intelligence is not knowledge but imagination."
-Albert Einstein

EXERCISE YOUR CREATIVITY

I find that when I frequently exercise my ability to be creative in different areas, creativity overflows into all areas of my life and helps me be innovative. Saving the planet against invisible aliens, building cardboard spaceships, and exploring the unknown on walks with my son exercises my creativity. Playing a video game, writing poetry, freestyling with friends, taking pictures, watching movies, are all activities that activate different parts of creativity in my brain. The result helps me live fully in whatever I do.

As a filmmaker, there are times I will work in corporate settings, filming interviews for clients. When I arrive in a room to film, I have to figure out the best place for our subject to sit that will look good on camera, with limited time. Sometimes I have to become an interior designer and rearrange a room so that it looks good – especially if the room is plain. After the shot is set up, I have to skillfully light the subject with lights and use shadows. At times, even when everything is set during production, things don't always go according to plan, and I have to think on my toes. I accredit creativity to my continual success on set. No matter what challenges you face, there is always a way to win with creativity.

Is there something you can do that will exercise your creativity? If you are focused only on "adult things," you are going to find yourself unmotivated, grumpy, and short on ideas. Here are some activities that will help with divergent thinking:

- Taking a walk to improve original ideas, learning and memory.[9]
- Physical exercise to improve creative thinking and problem solving.[10]
- Playing to improve imagination and innovation.[11]

This short list is to jump-start ideas for you. There are many more ways to improve and exercise your creativity including reading, listening to music, meditating, eating good food, and proper sleep. You may find some of these exercises really fun, so you can incorporate them into your daily schedule. (Fun shouldn't be reserved only for the weekends.) Where in your schedule can you make time to activate different parts of your brain? Sometimes, "adult" activities all day long can drain you. It is hard to create when you are under pressure and stressed out. Stress is a creativity killer. You need to be inspired!

RECREATE TO RE-CREATE

If you ever find yourself looking at a blank screen, drawing blanks, it's because you haven't had time to stop and smell the roses. You must recreate (enjoy life) to re-create (create anew). When you spend time doing different activities and hanging out with great company, ideas just sneak up on you because you're in a place of peace. The secret to brilliance is found in fun, rest, and peace. Why is it that the best ideas come when you are in the shower, driving, having fun or when you least expect it? Because you're at a place of rest and relaxation, free from worry and strife. Look for ways you can recreate. You will create anew!

> *"Creativity grows out of two things: curiosity and imagination."*
> ***-Benny Goodman, American clarinetist***

AVOID PERFECTIONISM

When you operate creatively, you may have to confront perfectionism at times. It hisses, "This isn't good enough. It can be better." How many of us are waiting too long to take a step of faith because we are waiting for the perfect moment or perfect product?

The most common excuses that hold people back have direct ties to perfectionism. For example:

- I don't have enough time
- I'm not ready
- I'm not qualified
- I don't have enough money

No one is ever ready. Everyone always has second thoughts and personal criticism. However, it is important to understand that nothing is perfect. So why wait to create or launch when you get better with everything you do? Reid Hoffman, the founder of LinkedIn said, "If you're not embarrassed by the first version of your product, you've launched too late." Being embarrassed doesn't necessarily mean you are unhappy with your creation. It just means you are committed to putting what you have out there, and you're not afraid to improve it. Apps are released every day. Every app periodically updates its system and improves its design. App designers do not wait until they have the perfect product. They release a product that has room for improvement. Feedback is taken into consideration and improvements are made to make it a better product. This is the world we live in today. You shouldn't be afraid of releasing a project or shy away from feedback. How will you ever become better on your next revision or product? When you put something out in the world, you get wiser and better with every experience. It's practice! Every video that I make as a filmmaker is always better than the last because I have more experience.

Excellence is the opposite of perfectionism. It is the confidence to do the very best with what you currently have. It is the pride to see what you create and say, "this is good." It is the pursuit to be better with every opportunity you get. Excellence is believing in yourself and in your work. Don't wait for the perfect moment. Put your best foot forward and do the best with what you have. Someone in the world needs it!

STRATEGY SESSION

1. SCHEDULE CREATIVITY

Leonardo Da Vinci kept a notebook. In it he wrote a to-do list filled with curiosities and interests like: discover the measurement of Corte Vecchio (the courtyard in the duke's palace), draw Milan, ask about the measurement of the sun, and examine the Crossbow of Mastro Giannetto. He always found a way to exercise creativity in his daily schedule. Is there anything you can do that will similarly exercise your sense of wonder? Can you draw, physically exercise, mediate, or use your imagination? Write down seven things you can do to boost your creativity this week. Schedule something for each day or you will never do it. Invest in your imagination. You will notice a difference.

2. CHALLENGE YOURSELF

Are you currently facing a problem or an obstacle that is within your power to fix? Think of three solutions to that problem. If you have board meetings at work, do not just present the problems, present alternative solutions along with them. This is how you practice thinking outside the box. Finally, challenge yourself to get 7-8 hours of sleep and eat food that is healthy for your body chemistry. Both these exercises will help to get the juices flowing.

3. GO FOR IT

What project have you put off that needs to be finished? Is it that book that needs to be published? Or a video that needs to be uploaded? Are you hesitant because it isn't perfect? Don't let perfection rob you! Being done is better than being perfect. Believe in yourself and in your work. Walk with excellence and do the best with what you have. Take the leap of faith and go for it.

CHAPTER 6:
SELF EDUCATION

*"Formal education will make you
a living; self-education will make
you a fortune." -**Jim Rohn***

I doubled my yearly income every year for four years straight running my video production business. My tax guy was impressed. Although it took hard work, I do not accredit my success to working harder. I worked smarter. It isn't hard to find inspirational speakers and motivational entrepreneurs talk about the importance of hard work on social media. You will hear quotes like "no days off" and "rich people don't sleep."

Sure, hard work is vital for success. But when was the last time you heard "work smarter, not harder"? Hard work alone isn't the recipe for success. If it was, those who have the hardest labor jobs would be the richest people on Earth. Those who put in the most hours would be the wealthiest. But this is simply not the case. Those who put hard work into working smarter will benefit the most.

The key to my success was investing in my personal and professional development.

SELF-EDUCATION

The more you learn, the more you can earn. Every time you acquire a new skill or make the skills you have better, you are investing in your professional value and earning ability. In his book, *NO Excuses! The Power of Self-Discipline*, Brian Tracy says, "Decide today to invest 3 percent of your income into yourself." So, if you make $40,000 a year, invest $1200 in yourself. Following this advice changed my life. When I started investing in myself, I began to work smarter and my earning ability began to rise. I invested in books, masterclasses, and training courses. I watched YouTube videos and listened to podcasts. I learned how to talk and market to the right client. I found out how to be productive with my time and how to take my skills to the next level. I discovered how to create better systems for my workflow and create a team. As I implemented what I learned, the payoff was incredible. By the end of the year, I realized I was able to double my yearly income running my business.

Jeff Sandquist, the General Manager of Microsoft once said, "If there was one change that Microsoft has made over the years that impacted our business the most, it was listening better to our customers. From that one change Microsoft started to take off. To constantly be improving, you have to be a LEARN IT ALL. Not know it all." Self-education should be a lifestyle. You will never grow if you think you already know everything. It is okay to rely on your expertise, as long as you are always willing to build upon what you know by learning more.

The more you learn, the more you can earn.

You can pick any available market and learn valuable skills on the internet. Most times you can find information for free. Robert Kawasaki, the author of *Rich Dad, Poor Dad* said in a recent interview on impact theory with Tom Bilyeu, "Your generation has the best teachers in the world. They're on YouTube; they're not in colleges." We live in a time where information is at the edge of your fingertips. With a click of a button, you can learn any skill you like on the internet – business, coding, taxes, sales, cooking, filming, anything you can think of. Whoever said, "you can't teach an old dog new tricks" didn't live in the age of information. You have more resources, tools, and road maps available to you then any generation before. Whether it be knowledge that is free or information that costs money, the most important investment you can make is in yourself. Are you willing to invest 3 percent of your income into your personal development? The payoff will be worth it.

CURIOSITY ENHANCES LEARNING

Like me, you may have done poorly in school. That's okay. Your GPA doesn't limit your potential nor does your performance in school have to dictate how far you can go in your earning ability. I spent time in school memorizing information just for it to evaporate after a test was over. If I wasn't interested in the subject, or had a boring teacher, it was hard for me to remember what was taught. But when it came to things I was interested in, like history, economics, and religion; I never forgot them.

The UC Davis Center for Neuroscience conducted research on how curiosity effects learning. They found that when you are interested about something, that curiosity enhances your ability to learn, increases brain activity, and retains the knowledge you find. "Curiosity may put the brain in a state that allows it to learn and retain any kind of information, like a vortex that sucks in what you are motivated to learn, and also everything around it," explains researcher Dr. Gruber.[12] You have the chance to educate yourself in the areas you are curious about right now. What are you interested in learning? There is no excuse for staying the same each year when there are so many options to upgrade yourself.

LEARN THE BEST WAY YOU KNOW HOW

The root word for education in Latin is edu-care, which means to "bring out," or "bring forth what is within." Your ability to learn new things will bring forth the seeds of greatness within you. Depending on how you learn, there are multiple ways this can happen. You can read a book. Don't like reading? You can listen to an audiobook or a podcast. Are you a visual learner? You can watch a tutorial or purchase an online course. Need group interaction? You can interact with others by joining a masterclass or attending a seminar, webinar, or social media group. If there is someone you admire in the field you aspire to join, see if they have any resources like books, podcasts or a YouTube channel.

> *"Take all the courses in your curriculum. Do the research. Ask questions. Find someone doing what you are interested in! Be curious!"*
> **–Katherine Johnson, NASA Mathematician**

If there are people you can network with in your field, ask them for advice. Most times, people don't seek out advice from others – whether it be the fear of rejection or intimidation. But, more often than not, successful people don't mind sharing their stories and what they learned along their journeys. If you can summon the courage to offer coffee or lunch for 15 minutes of their time, chances are you will get to spend more than 15 minutes with them. If they are hard to reach and very busy, one way to stand out in your request is to offer to pay them for their time as part of your personal development expenses. Bring a notepad, have your questions ready, and resist the urge to pick up your phone. Show them that their time is valuable by giving them your undivided attention. It will go a long way.

REACH OUT TO OTHERS

When I first started my business, I reached out to the top videographers in my field. All I had to do was ask around and look up top talent on social media. It wasn't long until I found talented professionals who mastered their craft. I would private message them and share that I would like to pay them for their time to simply ask questions. I either met with them in person or in Google chat. Here is an example of my initial private message:

Hey (person's name),

Thank you for taking the time to informally meet me here through Facebook. I own a video production company (www.experiormedia.com) here in the bay area. Although I have over 5 years of experience, I am always looking to learn. I have been in search of those at the top of the video production field and that is what brought me to you.

I have set apart money for my personal development and would love to sharpen my skill by meeting with you in person, or to google hangout, for a simple Q&A session. I would pay $50 an hour for your time. I am hungry to learn and would be honored if you would take time out for me. Please let me know if you are available for something like this.

Sincerely,
Joe Poni

From there I would send a follow up email with several dates for them to choose from, and we would meet for an hour. I would ask things like, "What's your story?" "How did you get into this?" "What are some of the most valuable lessons you learned along the way?" "How did you accomplish this or that?" "What do your daily routines look like?" "What motivates you to be disciplined?" and "What is your advice for someone just coming up in the business?"

Most times, this simple engagement will create an ally and expand your network. This strategy not only got me the chance to learn, but it also allowed me the opportunity to collaborate with the best in the business. After our conversations, friendships developed. Most people I reached out to gave me a shot to work with them on production sets. This is a practice I still use today.

Every year, you should aim to become better in some shape or form because whatever doesn't grow, ultimately dies.

APPLY YOUR KNOWLEDGE

It isn't enough to just learn and accumulate knowledge. The most important part of learning is execution. One of the problems with traditional higher education is the process to apply what you learn takes too long. On top of that, when you graduate, sometimes the information you studied is outdated. As you learn a new skill or attain new knowledge, it is imperative that you use it immediately. Read something good in a book? Talk about it to a friend. Watched a good tutorial? Replicate it. Learned something in a course? Implement it quickly. As you grow in your personal and professional development, you can become an asset to any organization by pushing yourself toward mastery. Every industry is in need of specific skills. If you can develop and master the skill set that is needed, you can become indispensable to your workplace. The same goes for expertise. If you can study and improve the knowledge you have of your industry, you can differentiate yourself from everyone else. As the market gets more competitive, your skills and wisdom will make you either stand out or blend in. Give yourself permission to stand out from the rest.

STRATEGY SESSION

1. LEARN SOMETHING NEW

There is more information available to us then any generation in history. Books, conferences, masterclasses, and podcasts, just to name a few, are all assessable at our fingertips. Is there a course that you can take to elevate your current skills or knowledge? Is there new technology you can learn that will help you in your field? There are different forms of learning you can take advantage of. Develop a growth mentality today and learn something new!

2. REACH OUT TO OTHERS

Is there anyone in your network you admire? Can you think of three people you can learn from that can help you on your journey? What is it about their life that stands out to you? Summon the courage to reach out to one of them this week. Ask them about their story.

3. DOES A SIDE HUSTLE INTEREST YOU?

You may not use all your skills in the occupation you have. Instead of leaving your gifts unused, start a side hustle. The economy is booming for those that can monetize their skill. According to a 2019 study,[13] 57 million Americans are doing freelance work today, which represents 35% of the U.S. workforce. That means that one-third of American workers are using their skill to earn extra revenue. This study also finds that free-lancers earn a median rate of $28 an hour. "Earn-ing more per hour than 70 percent of workers in the overall U.S. economy." Take a look around you. What skills are in demand right now? Are they skills you have? Are there skills you can learn? You can monetize your skills using on-line platforms as a side hustle.

4. LOOK INTO PASSIVE INCOME

I hired an electrician to hang up some lights in my backyard. He reconfigured an outlet outside and hung up the lights with ease. He is the best at what he does. However, he is 62 years strong. His time and labor equals his income. He has about 6-8 more years of hard labor before he hangs up his tool belt. Millions of people are just like him. They work for a living but what happens when they stop working? There is a way to make money without using your time or energy. There are different avenues you can look into to earn money while you sleep, like developing an online course, investing money in a Roth IRA, real estate, publishing a book, selling stock photos or videos, or running a business that doesn't need continual attention. There are different ways that are suitable for everyone. Simply search online "Ways to make passive income" to see how you can start today.

PART 3:

SUSTAIN & FLOURISH

CHAPTER 7:

THE SECRET TO SUCCESS NO ONE IS TALKING ABOUT

"You'll never change your life until you change something you do daily. The secret of your success is found in your daily routine."
- John C. Maxwell

When I started my production company, I wanted to join the top 20% of income earners in my field of work. I looked up online what other freelance video production companies were making. I saw what I could potentially earn in a year, so I broke down the numbers of what to make every month, week, and day to hit that mark. I wrote down what clients I needed to get, and what my year needed to look like, every month, week, and day to earn such numbers.

For example, if you want to make $60,000 for the year, you will need to make:

$5,000 a month, which is

$1,250 a week, or

$178 a day

DEVELOPING A ROUTINE

I knew it was going to take hard work, focus, and discipline to achieve this goal. I wasn't afraid of the hard work; I was up for the challenge. However, I was a little concerned about living disciplined. Have you ever had a paper due but instead of doing it, you did other things you *"had to do,"* like check social media and watch that new episode on Netflix? Me too. That's as *disciplined* as I can be. I considered myself a spontaneous person and always viewed discipline and routine as constraining and boring.

Although I dreaded the thought of routine, I noticed I already had one, and it wasn't a good one either. I would wake up, reach for my phone, check my social media, emails, and slowly roll out of bed onto my day. I would take on the day as it came, went to work, knocked out tasks that needed my attention, got home, spent time with the family, and tried to work out by the end of the night. My routine needed an upgrade. I knew I had to make some adjustments to maximize my productivity.

Just because we all have the same number of days in a year doesn't mean we are all able to fulfill what is in our hearts. Not everyone achieves what is important to them. The secret to accomplishing your heart's desires is developing a good routine. Productive daily routines and agendas put us on track to manifest our dreams. No one talks about routine. People usually encourage you to "ditch the routine and get the life you want!" However, I've noticed that developing a routine for my life has made my life exciting. My life changed when I developed a daily routine. I had time for everything – especially for what was important to me. All I did was factor everything into an agenda. No longer did I take the day as it came. I had a plan in place. I quickly realized having a routine wasn't bad; it was actually fun and fulfilling. Especially as I began to complete the desires that were in my heart. My goal was to join the top 20% of income earners in my field of work. With a routine in place, not only did I reach my target number, but I surpassed it. The most important adjustment I made was the first hour of my day.

The secret to accomplishing your heart's desires is developing a good routine.

THE MOST IMPORTANT HOUR OF YOUR LIFE

Your morning will set the tone for your day, and your days will shape the rest of your life. I found that I am ready to tackle the biggest responsibilities when I plan my day the night before. My daily routine started with writing a to-do list the night before and tackling the biggest task first thing in the morning. Writing a to-do list at night is also beneficial if you find yourself thinking too much before going to bed. I found that when I write out what I have to do for the next day, I get those pesky thoughts out of my head and sleep more peacefully.

This is what is called the "Ivy Lee Method (for achieving peak productivity)." The idea is at the end of each workday, write down the most important things you need to accomplish tomorrow. I usually write down three in order of importance, then wake up and complete them if possible. Adjusting the first hour of my mornings to tackle my day, changed the outcome of my year. You may not need to adjust the first hour of your day. You may need to adjust only the first 30 minutes. Make it happen. As John C. Maxwell said, "If you can figure out the best possible way to spend four, eight or twelve hours, you can be successful." The reason why planning your day is important is because if you don't focus on something, you will be distracted by everything. If you set apart time to do a task, it is important that you are fully immersed in the task and not distracted from your focus.

SOCIAL MEDIA APPS

If you've ever suffered from an inability to focus, you are not alone. One of today's difficulties is being able to direct our attention for long, uninterrupted periods of time. The main culprit responsible for these distractions may be our smartphones. Once you sit down, you can get a notification, email, update alert, text message, and a miss call all within 10 minutes. *And that is not an exaggeration.* We all know we can spend too much time on our phones. Especially on social apps. In his book *Digital Minimalism*, Cal Newport shares, "Most of the people who struggle with the online part of their lives are not weak willed or stupid. They're instead successful professionals, striving students, loving parents; they are organized and used to pursuing hard goals. The compulsive desire to check your phone is not a personal flaw, it is a software design created by software developers to keep you engaged with their product."

No one signs up for compulsive behavior when they download the latest social media app. But app developers design their platforms like slot machines. They want you to be hooked and keep coming back. Sean Parker, Facebook's first president, told Axios in an interview, "The thought process that went into building these applications, Facebook being the first of them, … was all about: 'How do we consume as much of your time and conscious attention as possible?' and that means that we need to sort of give you a little dopamine hit every once in a while, because someone liked or commented on a photo or a post or whatever." In other words, the goal of every app engineer is to program your brain, so you never get off its application.

REMASTERING FOCUS

Your ability to focus is one of your superpowers. This is why you must practice restraint and establish boundaries with apps. Social media isn't wrong. These platforms can be used to make income, connections, and lasting memories. However, in order to be effective in accomplishing greatness, you must turn your attention to deeper work. On my journey of creating a daily routine. I put in place boundaries with my apps so I can get work done and focus more. I set aside blocks of uninterrupted time when I need to concentrate and focus. If you make money from your social media posts, setting blocks of uninterrupted time will help you be more creative in delivering fresh content. Not only will you be clear-minded, but you will break compulsive habits and your productivity will increase as you meet your goals.

> *"Be less curious about people and more curious about ideas."*
> *–Marie Curie, Physicist and Chemist*

LEGACY

A survey by Tony Campolo, a sociology professor and speaker, asked people over the age of 90 if they could live life again, what would they do differently? The top three answers were stunning. They were:

- Risk more.
- Reflect more by "thinking where was my life going?"
- Do more things that will outlive me.

Have you taken time to think about where your life is going lately? What about the legacy you want to leave behind? Or are you just consumed with the fear of missing out on what someone will post next? Eleanor Roosevelt once said, "Great minds discuss ideas; average minds discuss events; small minds discuss people." Have you reduced your conversations to comments and posts instead of ideas and innovations? Are you so busy with the insignificant that you don't have time for what's really important? At the end of our lives you will not wish you spent more time watching TV or on your phone. You will wonder if you made a dent in the universe. Focus on doing more things that will outlive you and leave a legacy.

STRATEGY SESSION

1. CREATE A ROUTINE

"Every morning, I will wake up and stretch." "I will go for a walk for 15 minutes each day in the morning." "Every day at 5 p.m. I have to go to the gym." These are all examples of routines. You do not have to create an extensive routine for your day. It can be as simple as incorporating one activity in your day that you enjoy or need to do religiously. Is there something that is important to you? Quiet time? Reading? Exercising? How can you incorporate it into your day? Try it for 21 days. See what it feels like to have a routine.

2. WRITE DOWN A TO-DO LIST

Write down your to-do list the night before. Arrange your to-do list in the order of importance. Wake up and crush it.

3. TAKE TEN MINUTES TO GET STARTED

If you feel unmotivated for a particular task, all you need is ten minutes to get you into the flow. According to INC., "Getting started is usually the toughest part of any task. And the ten-minute rule is the key to getting started." The ten-minute rule is putting all your focus and energy into doing a task, and at the end of that ten minutes deciding whether to keep going. Nine times out of ten, you'll decide to keep going long past the 10 minutes."[14]

4. SET UNINTERRUPTED TIME

Being constantly interrupted can have ill effects on your brain and IQ. In 2005, Dr. Glenn Wilson conducted research at London's Institute of Psychiatry and found that persistent interruptions and distractions at work by emails and phone calls saw a 10-point fall in individuals' IQ.[15] Can you set apart uninterrupted time in your days? My uninterrupted time is in the mid-morning and afternoon. If I need to respond to calls or texts, I respond before or after. What does uninterrupted time look like to you? No phone past 6 p.m.? A sabbath day from technology? Review your activity log on your phone. What app do you spend the most time on? Is all that time needed? If you need to make some adjustments, write down what are the best times throughout your day to carve out for mental breaks. Disable notifications and set healthy boundaries with your apps and phone for productivity and focus.

5. PEAK PERFORMANCE

As an entrepreneur, I work from home a majority of the week, and it is imperative I operate at my peak performance. Although I exercise and get enough sleep, I would still feel sluggish on certain days. As my productivity increased, I could no longer ignore why I felt tired some days. I quickly realized my diet wasn't providing me with the proper nutrition I needed to perform at my peak. Something had to change. I saw a nutritionist, who took my blood, saliva, and gave me a summary report. The report was a written analysis of the foods that were good for my digestive system and blood. When I incorporated her advice, my life changed within weeks.

How is your performance? Are you working at your peak or do you find it difficult to make it through your days? Can you incorporate drinking more water in your diet and staying alkalized? You do not have to find a nutritionist, but if it interests you, set aside time to see one. Find out which foods you should be eating to improve your performance. Exercise. Sleep. Take mental breaks throughout your day. You only get one body. Take care of it.

CHAPTER 8:

THE IMPORTANCE OF RELATIONSHIPS

"You are the average of the five people you spend time with."
-Jim Rohm

Behavior is contagious. Spending time with world changers and those who get stuff done can transform your habits, mindset, and disciplines. Nobody becomes a success by themselves. Getting around people who will inspire you, challenge you, and encourage you can be what you need to excel. The narrative of being self-made simply isn't true. Even the greats had people that helped them to greatness. Steve Jobs had Steve Wozniak. Bill Gates had Paul Allen. Michael Jordan had Scottie Pippen and the Chicago Bulls. Good relationships are vital for our growth and greatness. Sure, you must put in the hard work to get to where you want to go; no one can do that for you. However, great relationships awaken the seeds of destinies within us.

Norman Triplett conducted a study with cyclists in 1898. He discovered that the cyclists who raced together were faster than those who raced alone. Like those cyclists, you need to be surrounded by others who can push you toward your destinies. The question you need to ask yourself is, who are you surrounded by?

MEETING GABE

When I got into filming, I knew I had to spend time around someone who was where I wanted to be professionally. I had to find that electric environment that made me come alive. I began to ask around and put myself out there to find someone who was already in my field and crushing it. That is how I met Gabe. When we first met, it was on the streets of Stockton through our mutual friend Oscar. I shared with Gabe how I was just starting out and was hungry to learn everything I could about filming. Not only did we become friends, but he invited me to be on a production set when he was producing a commercial. I soaked it all up and learned so much. I met so many amazing people on set that I am still friends with today. In the early months of my business, I would be lost on proposals, invoices, taxes, and how much to charge clients. I remember calling Gabe, and no matter what he was doing, would take the time to answer. I recall hanging on his every word as I took notes – knowing my success was in the balance. During my first year of business, Gabe gave me my first big shot when he referred a client to me. The night before production, I couldn't sleep. My nerves kept me up. I also started to feel under the weather, but nothing could stop me. I arrived on set, and the shoot was a success. That project put me on the map and led to so many more opportunities. Our friendship has been a blessing to me. It has also challenged me to go to the next level.

Nobody becomes a
success by themselves.

GOOD PEOPLE ARE GOOD FOR YOUR SOUL

Harvard University conducted the longest study on people to find out what leads to healthy and happy lives. This study began in 1938 and followed the lives of 268 people. Robert Waldinger, the director of the study, shared the research in his 2015 TED talk, "What Makes a Good Life? Lessons from the Longest Study on Happiness." He points out that "People who are more connected socially, live longer," and "the people

who were the most satisfied in their relationships at age 50 were the healthiest at age 80."
According to this research, just as good relationships keep us healthier and happier, loneliness
destroys our bodies as much as smoking and
alcoholism. Don't let business or pride hinder
you from a happy life. Make time for good relationships. It is good for the wellbeing of your
soul.

When you find the people you resonate with,
you discover your tribe. A tribe isn't people
who look like you or think like you. They are
anybody you vibe with who pushes you to your
destinies. They are the ones who challenge and
inspire you to be better. You may have yet to
find your community. Don't be discouraged.
Keep looking. If you feel like you don't have a
friend, become the friend you want. Celebrate
victories. Mourn losses. Be encouraging. Let it
start with you. When finding a community, look
for ways to be a blessing. In today's culture, everything is about me and what I can get. Sometimes relationships are built on sand because
they are based on what you can do for me, instead of what I can do for you. Great friendships
grow from life exchange. Whether personal or
professional, growth takes place when we give
the proper attention, respect, and support the
relationship deserves. We all need people. Lone
wolves never make it as far as those in a pack.
Surrounding yourself with good people is essential. Behavior, emotion, work ethic, are all
contagious. Authors of the book *Connected* ex-

plain, "One biological mechanism that makes emotions and behaviors contagious may be the so-called mirror neuron system in the human brain." In other words, if you see a behavior long enough, you can start to adopt it.

If you are the average of the five people you spend time with, that means if you hang out with five millionaires you will be the sixth. In the same fashion, if you hang out with five low-lifes, you will be the next addition.

BAD RELATIONSHIPS

Naysayers, doubters, and negative people also affect you negatively. You may be surrounded by relationships that you have outgrown. Some may have turned toxic, while other relationships are too demanding, leaving no time for your personal space or mental health. If this is the case, you may have to set up healthy boundaries.

DEVELOP HEALTHY BOUNDARIES

Boundaries are personal limits you set with people for your mental, emotional, and physical health. In neighborhoods, people create fences to protect their personal property. They keep out who they want out and those allow in have been given permission. You must have the same mindset when it comes to your well-being. The purpose of setting boundaries is to keep you healthy physically, emotionally, and mentally by being a good steward of your time and personal space.

You have the freedom to think, have opinions, and make decisions for yourself without the interference of another's control over you. If a relationship has run its course, you have the right to cut it off. For the relationships that you can't end easily, you should set up a boundary. You may have experienced someone who is demanding, controlling, or criticizing. That's why you must take responsibility because if you don't, they will. You do not need to feel guilty for setting boundaries with overbearing family members, friends, or co-workers.

John C. Maxwell once said, "Learn to say 'no' to the good so you can say 'yes' to the best." When you say "no" to something, it is because you're saying "yes" to something more important. Do not buy into the myth that you are being selfish for telling someone no. There is a difference between being selfish and being a steward. You are responsible for being a good steward with your life, priorities, and responsibilities. If people perceive that as selfish, that is none of your business.

DON'T FALL INTO GUILT TRIPS

People can be extreme or upset when you set up boundaries. They can use guilt trips to get their way. They may say things like:

- "If you really cared, you would do this for me."
- "I never ask you for anything and when I finally do, you are busy."
- "If I die, then maybe you will care."
- "Come on, we never get to hang out."
- "You owe me."

You can't control what people say or their reactions and emotions. However, you can control your actions and emotions. Healthy boundaries will help you protect your well-being.

MY STORY

When I was in college, I couldn't get a handle on my life. My problem was that I was trying to please everyone, and I didn't want to let anyone down. I ended up living my life based on what other people thought my life should look like instead of how I felt called to live it. When I decided to incorporate healthy boundaries, I found myself living the life I wanted. I traveled, invested in my personal education, and started to focus on my personal curiosities. Setting boundaries does not get you out of responsibilities or isolate you. Boundaries just put you back in charge with your life, and that's exactly what I did.

As you navigate through life, you will meet all sorts of people. Learning how to find your tribe, seek mentors, and set healthy boundaries will be key to your growth.

STRATEGY SESSION

1. FIND YOUR TRIBE

Even the greats had people that helped them to greatness. Are there people that are doing what you want to do? Do you have a way to spend time around them? You often find your community when you meet people you resonate with. When you find your tribe, you unlock the destinies within yourself.

2. BE ACCOUNTABLE

Are there people in your life walking alongside you? Is there anyone dependable and willing to show up in your life? They do not have to be your best friend or have all the answers. They could be people who provide accountability whom you respect. Who can you ask to be accountable to for your dreams? Find someone you can begin to meet with weekly or monthly that you can give an account of your goals or dreams.

3. BE A GOOD FRIEND

Is there someone you have in mind you can be a better friend to? Never fall into a trap of envy or jealousy when others are doing good. Who are some people you can encourage, believe in, celebrate? If you want good friends in your life, first become one.

4. PRACTICE HEALTHY COMMUNICATION

You can't prevent conflicts, arguments, and disagreements in your life, but you can prevent them from ruining your relationships. Learning to communicate how you feel can create good results in your relationships. Let's face it, we've all had situations that have turned sour because of miscommunication or because of a conflict gone wrong. Conflict doesn't have to be a bad thing. Conflict can actually create a deeper connection within your relationships, if handled correctly. The ways you shouldn't handle conflict are obvious: jealousy, bickering, fighting, and talking behind someone's back. Avoiding a conflict or a conversation by thinking it will handle itself isn't good either. It leaves room for bitterness and speculation to creep into your relationship. It is good to address conflicts as they arise by communicating as soon as you can. Here are some ways you can communicate and handle conflict in a healthy way:

1. Communicate calmly.

Have you ever tried to communicate when you were angry? I bet it didn't work out too well. Healthy confrontation isn't yelling your opinion. In the heat of the moment, it is good to take time for yourself and be at peace so you can convey your feelings calmly.

2. Talk in person or over the phone but not through text.

If you desire to resolve a conflict, texting isn't a good option. Texting is a good way to be misunderstood and have your words taken out of context, especially when addressing an important issue.

3. Understand one another.

A good way not to take things personally is to put yourself in the other person's shoes. If you can make understanding your goal in confrontation and not the need to be right, you can eliminate back-and-forth arguing.

4. Your feelings and their feelings are valuable.

In conflict, it is better to share how you feel instead of pointing the finger. (Especially if it's the middle one!) Letting a person know "I feel _____ when you _____" is a good way to convey your feelings.

5. Listen and respond with love.

Genuinely hear people out. Be open to the possibility that you may be wrong. If so, humble yourself. You will find out that when you listen well, sometimes the issue isn't as big of a deal as you thought it was. Whatever the case may be, be ready to forgive, forget, and respond with love.

5. SET HEALTHY BOUNDARIES

We all have equal time in a day. But if you don't manage your time, others will. According to the authors of *Boundaries*, "Boundaries are personal property lines that are physical, mental, and emotional to help you prioritize your life." Is there anyone you need to set boundaries with? Is there anyone you should stop accepting guilt from? Setting boundaries is necessary throughout your life. It can be in person or via internet. For instance, if there is someone you are following on social media that is causing you to self-analyze or posts comments that discourage you, you should set a healthy social media boundary and unfollow or delete.

CHAPTER 9:
DEFY THE ODDS

*"The two most important days in
your life are the day you are born
and the day you find out why."*
-Mark Twain

I can still remember the reactions I would get every time I would mention I went to a continuation high school. It was almost as if people were shocked to hear the news. Women would hold their purses closer; men would tell their family to get into the car as they locked their doors and drove off. And I'm just describing my relatives. I got into a fight in the principal's office and was expelled as a sophomore. This was my second time being expelled. The unfortunate thing about these situations is seeing the school counselors, vice principals, and board members for expulsion hearings puts you in a negative light, and my record didn't help. My grades were bad, my attendance was horrible, and I got in trouble with the law. This is what brought me to continuation school. However, my trajectory changed before it was time to graduate. I went from earning D's and F's to A's and B's. I graduated with seven scholarships and gave a speech on stage. I went on to become an inspirational speaker in the same school district that expelled me. To this day, I do workshops and offer scholarships in my name to help students striving to succeed. Professionally, I went on to own a video production company that has done commercials for some of the top brands in Silicon Valley. But if you sat in my expulsion hearings in high school, you would have doubts about my future and career trajectory. So, what changed?

My identity.

YOU BECOME WHAT YOU BELIEVE

As the famous saying goes: "As a man thinkth, so he shall be." What you believe about yourself is what you will become. Your behavior will always follow your beliefs. Transformation takes place when you renew your mind of negative, disempowering thoughts to thoughts that are filled with hope and optimism. You cannot expect something good with bad thinking. Your focus must bring you to a place of empowerment. If your thinking brings you to a place you don't like, then you need to exchange those thoughts with new ones. It is your mindset that creates good or bad days. A negative mindset can strip you of the power you need for today. This is why you must confront your assumptions and examine if your thoughts are serving you in becoming the person you want to become.

MOVE PAST YOUR PAST

In middle school, I found myself not having fun on the weekends. All I thought about was going back to school on Monday. I was bullied. I was the new kid in school and looked handsome, with the nicest eyebrows. No wonder all the guys were jealous. My stomach would turn walking down the hallways wondering what I was going to face that day. I remember crying in the mornings, begging my mom to let me stay home from school. She would cry and encourage me that it would get better. I planned on dropping out in 8th grade because it was so bad. I would get into fights, get suspended, and would eventually have to switch schools.

Getting in trouble and hearing things from teachers like, "you are wasting your time" and "you won't last long here" made me believe I wasn't good enough. I started to become the stereotypes others thought of me. My grades began to plummet because of the negative names and labels I adopted for myself. I stopped taking education seriously and because of that, I didn't know how to read. One of my best friends thought I would pretend to stutter in middle school just to make everyone laugh. He asked me in college one day, "Joe, remember when you used to pretend you didn't know how to read in 8th grade?" I told him "Jay, I wasn't pretending. I really didn't know how to read!" I guess I played it off like a pro.

Maybe it was a parent who said something negative to you. Maybe it was a sibling, classmate, or a co-worker that said something cynical. Their words do not have to have power over you any longer. Their actions can't keep you from who you are called to be.

CHANGE YOUR TRAJECTORY

Eleanor Roosevelt once said, "No one can make you feel inferior without your consent." If you have given someone power over you in the past, it is time to take it back. You do not have to get permission from nay-sayers or negative people on how far you can go in life. You must resist the temptation to feel sorry for yourself, and instead do something with your life. Do not fall into a victim-mentality trap. Life can be hard. You will face difficulty either because of your ethnicity, financial condition, mistakes, unexpected tragedy, or something else. Whatever the case may be, it is not what happens to you, that determines the quality of your life, it is your response that defines your future. You must take ownership of your outcomes. You are not a victim. You are called to defy the odds. Your past doesn't have to define you. You choose what defines you. You choose your trajectory. You choose who you will become.

Shawna Bertlin, the creator of activate identity at the University of Idaho says, "The person you are becoming is more important than who you have been."

So, who do you want to become? Once you decide who you want to be, you can take action to solidify your identity. People of great value live by great values. Honesty, commitment, empathy, patience, sacrifice, hard work, and determination are some values that make a noble character. When you begin to incorporate these or other good attributes into your life, they can have a powerful effect on who you are. It takes practice with every decision you make and interaction you have. When I struggled with reading comprehension, in order to change that reality, not only did I believe I could be better, but I had to practice. I have read over 500 books, and today I am an author.

You are called to defy the odds.

IDENTITY

Too often we base our identities and values in the wrong things. We form identities on what we do and how we look. However, when those things change, we can feel devalued or face an identity crisis. Your value doesn't come from the car you drive, how much you have in the bank or by the interactions on a social media post.

You are valuable because you were created as a masterpiece. There is no one on this planet that can be another you. You are truly one of a kind. You are important because you can make your world a better place. This is why you are valuable. You may need a reminder at times, but that comes from people you can trust like a grandparent, a good mother, father, or a positive mentor.

REINVENT YOURSELF

People evolve every year. Physically, you evolve daily. Each day your cells are renewing themselves. For example, you get new skin cells every two-to-four weeks. That means you are being renewed from who you were into who you are becoming. You are not the same person you were a year ago, a week ago, or a day ago. Every day is a chance for a fresh start with a new beginning.

Technology is also always updating. Whether you have a phone or an app, systems require updates as products advance, evolve, or incorporate customer feedback. Just like your phone, you need to update your system. You need to replace negative thoughts with empowering thoughts. Every day you have a chance to reinvent yourself into the person you want to be. Reinvention is needed when you experience changes like starting a new job, leaving a relationship, moving to a new location, or losing someone you love. When shifts take place in your life, you need to learn how you can use it to strengthen and make yourself better, not worse.

Every adversity has its own advantage. Sometimes it is the tough things of your past or present that shape you for the great things in your future. Reinvention takes time and patience. The great Jazz trumpeter and composer Miles Davis once said, "Sometimes it takes you a long time to sound like yourself." If you are committed to becoming all that you can be, shedding your old skin is a must. Don't live in the box that people put you in. Don't conform to what others think you should be. Be you. The world needs who you are. So, who will you become?

STRATEGY SESSION

1. CHANGE YOUR TRAJECTORY

Eleanor Roosevelt once said, "No one can make you feel inferior without your consent." What labels or stereotypes do you have to confront to establish your truest identity? Exchange one negative thought about yourself with an encouraging thought. You will break free from destructive patterns when you believe a better narrative about yourself.

2. FORGIVE OTHERS

People will wrong you. They will also disappoint you. The antidote is forgiveness. Forgiveness is powerful. Often times, forgiveness is mistaken for trust. But they are not the same. If I had a dollar and you took it without my permission, I can forgive you, but I don't have to trust you around my wallet. Holding grudges and not forgiving others can prohibit you from being emotionally healthy. The right decision is to set up healthy boundaries and move forward better, not bitter.

3. PROTECT YOUR IDENTITY

Your identity should not be rooted in what you do, how you look, where you live, or what you have. If your identity is wrapped up in your career, when what you do stops or changes, you can be vulnerable to depression, stress, or an identity crisis. The same goes for appearance. If you get your identity from the way you look, when your appearance evolves, your self-esteem can shatter. Our identity and self-worth should always rest inside, knowing that simply being you is enough. You're valuable because you are alive, and you always have something special to offer the world. Validation shouldn't come from things that fade. You may need a reminder of your identity at times, but that comes from people you can trust. Can you name three people who can remind you of your truest identity and challenge you to be better?

CONCLUSION

You were born for such a time as this. You weren't made to just make a living; you were made to make a difference. Do not worry that you will somehow be left behind. You are alive during the best time in history. The world is waiting for you. Bring solutions, use creativity, innovate, adapt, ruffle some feathers, raise your earning ability, find your tribe, master your skills, and defy all odds!

Separate yourself from an apathetic life. Hold fast to the fire within you. You were created to make your world a better place. As long as you have breath in your lungs, you have a purpose in your soul. Explore the great unknown. Follow your curiosity.

BONUS CHAPTER:
IDENTIFY YOUR CALLING

"Your career is what you're paid for. Your calling is what you're made for." -Steve Harvey

In society, we primarily associate the term "work" in reference to our job or our career. We say things like "I have to go to work," or "I have work to do," usually referring to a nine-to-five. However, "work" can refer to something greater than an occupation. The word vocation comes from the Latin word vocare, which means "to call." A "calling" refers to work that has a strong inclination toward a mission or responsibility that will benefit others. Being a parent, leaving an inheritance, writing a book, feeding the hungry, fighting for civil rights, starting a non-profit and helping the sick or elderly are all examples of different callings people feel. A calling is the inward conviction you cannot ignore. It is the work you do that makes the world around you a better place.

DIFFERENCE BETWEEN CAREER AND CALLING

There is a difference between career and calling. Your career is what you are employed to do. Your calling is what you are deployed to do. Your career is what makes a living. Your calling is what makes a difference. The famous painter, Vincent Van Gogh once said, "Your profession is not what brings home your paycheck. Your profession is what you were put on Earth to do, with such passion and such intensity that it becomes your spiritual calling." What are you put on this Earth to do? Do you feel any specific calling on your life?

What are you put on this earth to do?

RESOURCE YOUR CALLING

That being said, your career and calling can be related. There are times your career can give you the resources you need to pursue a calling on your life. In 2018, NBA champion LeBron James opened the I Promise School, an elementary school for at risk youth in his old neighborhood in Akron, Ohio. Students receive free uniforms, meals, Chromebooks, and a free bicycle and helmet. Those who graduate from the program and promise to work hard toward their high school diploma receive free tuition at the University of Akron.

Sharing about the launch of his school, LeBron said, "Everything these kids are going through – the drugs, the violence, the guns, everything they're going through as kids, I know. For me to be in a position where I have the resources, the finance, the people, the structure and the city around me - why not?" LeBron's career provided the resources to do what was in his heart, to give back to his community.

HOW TO IDENTIFY YOUR CALLING

You may not know where to start or what having a calling feels like. That's okay. A perfect place to start is by identifying simple clues in your life that bring you conviction or compassion. These are the magnets that draw you toward your true work. You can also have multiple callings in your life. Some missions are lifelong, while others will come and go. Many people throughout history have had multiple callings/vocations. Take Elon Musk for example. His conviction led him to explore space, advance research for the human brain and engineer better vehicles for the environment. He is living out his callings and getting paid to do it. Are you moved with conviction or compassion for anything? What are you put on this Earth to do?

Instead of wondering what you were born to do in the future, find what you are supposed to do right now. As soon as you know, give it your all.

STRATEGY SESSION

1. LOOK FOR CLUES

The clues of certain life callings are often hidden within our past. At an early age I knew I was called to use my voice ever since my teacher put a sticker on my shirt in the first grade that said, "chatter box." They may seem comical, but it is the little confirmations that help you pinpoint your personal callings. I have always loved to talk, and I knew it was something I was supposed to do. Likewise, writing this book was something I felt called to do. Being a dad was something I felt called to be. Identifying callings in your life can help you live life on purpose instead of by accident. Here are some questions to awaken different callings for your life:

- What gave you a sense of purpose in your past?
- What did you want to be or do when you were a child?
- What legacy would you like to leave behind for your family and your community?
- What is one thing you want to do that can benefit others?

For some, a career and a calling can intercept. Their profession can align with their purpose. For most, it may not be realistic to find a career that incorporates your calling. However, you can still make time for your callings. Can you schedule time for the work you feel called to do?

2. WHAT DOES YOUR PAST TELL YOU?

When you overcome obstacles, you have the grace to help others going through the same things you have conquered. Having a calling is helping your world become a better place. Here are additional questions to identify different callings for your life:

- What painful experience have you endured that you can help others get through?
- What breaks your heart in society? Is there something you can do about it?
- If you had unlimited resources, what problem would you solve?

You may need to spend some time pondering these questions as you answer them. Write them down in your journal. See if something clicks. If you felt something come to mind, take heed. This is how callings are formed.

CAN YOU HELP ME?

Thank you so much for reading my book! I would greatly appreciate your feedback and hearing what you have to say. Please leave me an honest review online to let me and others know what you thought of the book.
Thank you again!

Joe Poni

ENDNOTES

Chapter 1 FOLLOW YOUR CURIOSITY

1   https://www.newsweek.com/creativity-crisis-74665
2   https://www.syndacast.com/video-marketing-statistics-trends-2015/

Chapter 2 REIMAGINE YOUR POSSIBLITIES

3   https://reports.weforum.org/future-of-jobs-2016/chapter-1-the-future-of-jobs-and-skills/
4   Stanley, T.J. The Millionaire Next Door: The Surprising Secrets of America's Wealthy, p. 4
5   https://www.huffingtonpost.com.au/2017/10/18/weve-broken-down-your-entire-life-into-years-spent-doing-tasks_a_23248153/

Chapter 4 DISRUPTERS

6   https://www.ibtimes.com/sad-end-blockbuster-video-onetime-5-billion-company-being-liquidated-competition-1496962
7   https://www.businessinsider.com/rise-and-fall-of-blockbuster#but-trouble-was-on-the-horizon-in-1997-as-blockbusters-future-competitor-netflix-was-founded-7

Chapter 5 UNLOCK YOUR CREATIVITY

8   https://www.youtube.com/watch?v=ZfK-Mq-rYtnc
9   https://news.stanford.edu/2014/04/24/walking-vs-sitting-042414/
10   https://www.frontiersin.org/articles/10.3389/fnhum.2013.00824/full
11   https://www.pbs.org/newshour/science/the-secret-to-creativity-according-to-science

Chapter 6 SELF EDUCATION

12   https://www.cell.com/neuron/fulltext/S0896-6273(14)00804-6
13   https://www.upwork.com/press/2019/10/03/freelancing-in-america-2019/

Chapter 7 THE SECRET TO SUCCESS NO ONE IS TALKING ABOUT

14   https://www.inc.com/amy-morin/want-to-stop-procrastinating-try-the-10-minute-rule.html?fbclid=IwAR21ykZkFUxyb7Ye6OUsxnjl4fvLN_OmT1UBxoBF1exf8DvvtZCGnXU5qbA
15   https://www.theguardian.com/technology/2005/apr/22/money.workandcareers

Made in the USA
Monee, IL
29 May 2021

69048548R00075